THE POETRY GAMES

ESSEX

Edited By Connor Matthews

First published in Great Britain in 2018 by:

Young Writers
Remus House
Coltsfoot Drive
Peterborough
PE2 9BF
Telephone: 01733 890066
Website: www.youngwriters.co.uk

FOREWORD

Since 1991 our aim here at Young Writers has been to encourage creativity in children and to inspire a love of the written word. Each competition is tailored to the relevant age group, hopefully giving each pupil the inspiration and incentive to create their own piece of creative writing, whether it's a poem or a short story. We truly believe that seeing their work in print gives students a sense of achievement and pride.

For our latest contest The Poetry Games, secondary school pupils were given the challenge to stand up for what they believe in using nothing but the power of the pen. Using poetry as their tool, these aspiring poets were given the opportunity to express their thoughts and feelings on the topics that matter to them through verse. Using a variety of themes and styles, these featured poets leave a lasting impression of their inner thoughts and feelings, making this anthology a rare insight into the next generation.

We encourage young writers to express themselves and address topics that matter to them, which sometimes means exploring sensitive or difficult topics. If you have been affected by any issues raised in this book, details on where to find help can be found at: **www.youngwriters.co.uk/support.**

CONTENTS

William Brian Matthews (12) 86
Juwariyah Zubair (12) 87
Ritthyha Kumanan (12) 88
Chanel Kyei (13) 89
Tanisha Zaman (12) 90
Daeem Zaki (12) 91
Carlota Jesus (12) 92
Kaneez Fatima (12) 93
Rebekah Hughes (12) 94

Grays Convent High School, Grays

Cara Graca Chapatarongo (13) 95
Sara Ahmed (13) 96
Siân Kira Arkan (13) 100
Jodie Rae Fullerton (13) 102
Amreet Dhillon (13) 104
Jessica Westell (13) 106
Abigail Cosgrave (13) 107
Sanna Hashimi (13) 108
Niamh White (13) 109
Lily Rebekah Knights (13) 110
Aida Mataj (13) 111
Niamh Dennis (12) 112

Ormiston Rivers Academy, Burnham-On-Crouch

Ichabod Mills (16) 113
Megan Robinson (13) 114
Hannah Shelley (12) 115

Roding Valley High School, Alderton Hill

Skye Salek-Haddadi (12) 116
Poppy Tribe (11) 118
Carys Gooding (12) 119
Amber Elizabeth Compton (12) 120

Saffron Walden County High School, Saffron Walden

Anna Broadbent (12) 121

The Harris Academy, Rainham

Keira Star (12) 122
Caitlin Turner (13) 124
Melina Tiwari (14) 125
Mia Brown (12) 126
Alice Hope (12) 128
Immanuel Kotey (13) 130
Victoria-Enemwingue Idahosa- 131
Obazee (13)
Victor Adablah (13) 132
Alex Avery (13) 133
Kajus Proskinas (13) 134
Adrian Davidson (12) 135
Charlotte Luggar (11) 136
Jack Moorey (12) 138
Bethany Debono (13) 139

Thomas Lord Audley School, Monkwick

Elliot Crimes (13) 140
Ashleigh Oldfield (12) 142
Tyler Riley (13) 143
Megan Curtis (13) 144
Lana Hay (13) 145
Lewis Robert Bowyer (13) 146
Freddie Baker (13) 147
Aimee Georgina Wood (13) 148
Napat Menic Tawanyarat (13) 149

Westcliff High School For Girls, Westcliff-On-Sea

Oreoluwa Akinwunmi (13) 150
Ade Hikmat Kosoko (12) 151
Isabelle O'Dell (12) 152
Edward Maclannan-Brown (17) 154

THE POEMS

LONE WOLF

My pack left me to travel alone
So I step into another territory on my own
All eyes turn towards me as I walk down the hall
They point and jeer, I stand out like the oddball.

It's impossible I know, but I want to run away and hide
I lift up my shoulders and stare back with pride
Although I know I'll break down soon
I walk past them all like I own the moon.

The last bell goes and I run to my home
I drop all my things and hide in my dome
Sometimes I wish I had a magic potion
To search for them high and low over the ocean.

I never found them and went back to my memory
Which now feels like a whole century
To see them just once was all I could hanker
I felt like my heart was tied down with an anchor.

Aysha Hussain (13)

THE FRAGMENTED STATE OF MY MIND

Belligerently, sneering subconsciously is what my friends do
to each other when they are afraid
Afraid of what each other will think of them when their
weakness is revealed by the blade
Danger awaits, the truth is the sword to their secrets that
they protect with a durable shield
Frightened they are when the shield is lowered, so they sow
seeds of lies to protect them, which yield
Regrettably, they see a sea of flowers and to them only one
of them is more precious than rubies
Instantly the sword cuts through their grown plants of lies
and their concern for the future is broody
Envy, pride and arrogance are the physical foundation of
their satisfaction and their existence
Narcissistically, they stand firmly on a strong step structured
by deceit and wrongful persistence
Detonating what they think but surely... surely crude jokes
and sharing of memes cannot contribute towards euphoria
Showing consistent kindness and concern for each other for
them would be a literal dystopia

I'm a white sheet filled with dirty stains that can't be
removed no matter how hard I wash
My words can be repugnant and cannot be purified by
plentiful mouthwash

I'm an enigma squinting tirelessly, trying to comprehend the
blurred lines of my personality
Torrents of thoughts and emotions seal their place in my
body and take their hospitality
I'm a robot specifically programmed to perform algorithms
of procrastination
Perhaps in the future I can be productive and not be
naturally lazy which is a river of stagnation

My biological makers - I want to make them proud perhaps
playfully fly in the air for a living
But the costs are the thorns of a cactus which cause me to
bleed, which is not worth the sacrifice
They say that everyone is unique and different but I lie in a
highly populated of average
Surely, surely a multitude of people are intelligent I must
stand out and have courage
People are burdened with sorrows and woes which I want to
help them overcome
But stress is a silent killer devouring anyone who, to
excessive pressure, succumbs.

Clive Tinashe Matsiwe (15)

A SOLEMN STAR

One day, the sun sears the skin - a familiar feeling.
I return with a slip of paper, ravenously clawed from a wispy white envelope,
A bunch of letters and numbers to which you are alien.
My smile, your Rosetta stone; you peruse cluelessly.
Admitting defeat against the whirlpool of hieroglyphs, you smile, pride seeping from your kind lips.
Your tough hands emanate softness as they caress my warm hair.
I bend down, of course having outgrown your height years ago.
For a blissful moment, our orbits are level.
Another day, raindrops cascade down. Kissing the cold concrete.
A familiarly foreign feeling.
You open the door to my steel face.
Shivering, I slink in, a silent skeleton.
Words gush back down my throat, as I gesture for food.
Piping hot chicken curry and rice, you knew it was my favourite.
As I ate sombrely, you knew.
I stifled back the tides; you asked in a silky tone.
The monsoon arrived, raindrops cascaded onto my plate.
You were foreign to the words they fired or the reason they pulled the trigger.
Yet you knew, squeezing me tight, reclaiming me into your kind bosom, preventing me from bleeding out.

For a melancholy moment, our orbits were level.
Other days the sky is barren, cold and starless.
In my room I stay, held hostage by presumptions.
A fortress of textbooks, screens, insecurity, love and loss.
However, you break in with a smile every time, offering me chai.
Disregarding my facade of privacy, angst and ricocheting emotions.
With a ruffle of the hair I gelled for that one perfect picture, you leave smugly.
My superficial troubles scatter back into the shadows.
I'm content. For a blissful moment, our orbits are level as I bask in your warm rays.
Filled with a spark of determination, I hope that one day your son can be your sun.

Afzal Hussain (15)

ANOREXIA

Just like a pack of cigarettes
You came with the warning signs and the side effects
I took a breath
And I could breathe again
I swallowed your fumes
And I was whole again.

So much more than 'just a bad habit'
I drenched you in fuel
Yet I'm the one on fire?

Choking on clouds of smoky regrets
My lungs sink heavier in their cage
And with every intoxicated inhalation
More tangled thoughts twist together
Into the rope of torturous torment.

Dark fog clouds my once perfect vision
It stings my eyes and burns my lips
But the pain,
I crave it.

And so,
I'm falling
Down
Down

Down to the ground
Like the ashes that used to burn me.

I'm an addict, I'm out of control
Won't accept that you're making me sick
Because I'm oh so far from sick of you.

So I breathe you in just to breathe you back out again,
Until I am reduced to nothing but the butt of a burnt-out
cigarette.

Alice Bromell (17)

BOOKS

Books, books, where do I look?
I have towers and towers of books
Everywhere I look there are books.

My bed is made of books
My toilet is made of lots of books
My clothes are book-related
My mind is buzzing and twitching now
Writing this poem 'bout books.

I can't live without them
Those printed words on an ageing page
While threadbare on the covers...

Rebecca Green

MENTAL HEALTH

D o they ever know how it feels?

E ver heard the words, 'you're broken'?

P retending that you're okay

R eally though, everything is dark inside

E ven though you try to deny it

S ometimes you pretend you are normal

S o for that split second, you're happy again

I n your mind though, the truth still lurks

O ver again you repeat this process

N ever being able to escape the abyss.

S omeone who intentionally hurts themselves

E veryone who does it does it to express emotional distress

L iving is normally harder when you have this disorder

F or it's a kind of punishment.

H ave you witnessed someone self-harming?

A nd if you have, what have you done?

R eminded them everything is okay?

M aybe, but what good has that done?

Luca Magyar (12)
Anglo European School, Willow Green

THE SWING

The swing where they once sat
Stood alone under the sky
No more children, no more chat
The swing had been left to die.

Oh, but the stories
The swing had held
All the truths and the lies
All the names that have been spelt.

It remembers the girl
Who would come at 8
Through winter, through summer
Never early, never late.

She would tell about her day
She would tell about her thoughts
It got it thinking, she would stay
It hadn't learned from what it taught.

It remembers the boy
Who came every week
A new story to tell
With a smile on his cheek.

Yet all happiness and laughter
Must come to an end

As news had arrived
Of his descent.

The happy-go-lucky
A smile never left his face
Who knew
Tears could be found under the base.

All the stories it could tell
All the stories it knew well
All the people it had met
All the people came and went.

Despite the pain the swing had felt
With every person that went
It loved the stories, loved the new
As the feeling grew and grew.

Yet as the swing grew older
And its friends moved on
Everyone began to forget
About the lovely swingset they had met.

So as the swing hangs low
From the tallest tree
The more it realised
How lonely it had been.

The swing where they once sat
Sways gently with the wind
With no one there but its mind
The lonely swing had been left behind.

Anna Urbas (13)
Anglo European School, Willow Green

JUDGEMENT

The church tells everyone they're welcome
So why, if I'm a Muslim, can't I join?
Or if I'm a youth, people assume I steal or I'm out to cause trouble?
Why do people judge just from appearance?
It's like looking at a box and knowing what's in it.

People take one look at me and assume I'm gay
just because I'm wearing a pink shirt
So in their eyes, I'm gay
So I can't have a marriage at a church
As in some Christian views, I am not normal.

The news says they are honest and don't judge
So why have they shown me as a neglectful parent
Letting my kid fall out of a window, not caring?
But what they didn't know is how I did not let him fall
They took one look at me, saw my dirty hair and bloodshot eyes and assumed I was a neglectful parent.

Don't judge people from the outside, judge from the inside
Just like a birthday present, you don't care about the wrapping paper, just the present.

Morgan Harris (13)
Beauchamps High School, Wickford

LIFE

The path we take,
which defines our fate,
shouldn't be justified
because they've lied
about the blood
which floods our veins.

Everyone deserves to choose
whether they want to win, or lose.
No one should be segregated
because they've been themselves,
and still been hated.

We all breathe, sleep and eat
just like the people we meet.
So why when we fly into this world,
this world full of hate,
why do we close our minds like a gate?

Why is our life chosen for us,
just like Rosa Parks sitting on a bus?
and, why does it depend on the colour of our skin,
or whether we're fat or thin?
Why does it depend on the language we speak,
or the food we eat?
Why does it depend on the way we act?
And why do we all just turn our backs?

We blame all the disasters
on anyone we can find.
The feeling pierces through our minds.
It makes us believe that we are useless,
empowering our minds, telling us that we are worthless.

Millions of people think
if their lives are worth taking,
but they know they can't keep faking.
They shut their minds
and stop the thinking,
they wonder whether
they want to keep blinking.

Enough is enough,
we're powering through,
we are tough.
This hate won't break us down,
take a look and see these disappearing frowns.

Saskia Scarlett Warren (13)
Beauchamps High School, Wickford

REMEMBER

The light disappears
From her eyes,
Anger sets in
Because she can't remember a thing.

She didn't ask for this,
It wasn't her fault,
She's trapped in her own mind,
Unable to escape from herself.

She can't help it,
Just go along with it,
My own anger sets in with her,
Even if she can't help it.

Blank stares, glassy eyes,
Tired face, overworked brain,
Dementia took over
An assault on her brain.

She can barely remember me,
Confused looks and echoing words
As she echoes my name,
Like she's trying to remember who I am.

The vacant look
Tears me up inside

Breaks me like a mirror,
And yet I'm still angry.

"Can I go home?"
She doesn't know where home is,
She remembers parts of her past
But not enough to know where home is.

Hidden love behind a distant face
Is shadowed by nervousness and anger,
My own anger is hidden,
Deep down so no one sees.

My anger is aimed at everything:
Her, as she can't remember,
Me, as I can't help her,
But mainly the dementia
As that is the reason for my torment
And her loss of time and people.

Jessica King (14)
Beauchamps High School, Wickford

WASTING AWAY

Numbers dropping day by day,
Gradually taking her life away,
Her ribs stick out, the lines grow tighter,
Day by day, she gets lighter and lighter.

When the numbers start to rise,
Tears no longer stay dry in her eyes,
She won't give up until skin is tight,
Believing deep inside it's worth the fight.

But this was all caused by a high school bully,
Not thinking of how it would affect her fully,
All she wanted was to be a perfect winner,
But for this to happen she felt she must be thinner.

It takes half a second to call a girl fat,
But she will spend her whole life trying not to be that,
She will go too far to prove you wrong,

Until, one day, she is dead and gone.

Sophie Norris (13)
Beauchamps High School, Wickford

CHANGE

I aspire to be who I am,
Anyone who judges me is wrong,
Height doesn't mean anything,
Because it's what's inside that matters.

A man can decide his future,
No matter how big or small,
Anyone can make their dreams come true,
You just have to believe,
And not let anyone judge you,
Because if you don't,
Then anything is possible.

In society,
Opinions are changing,
Personalities are changing,
But you shouldn't,
Don't change because someone around you is,
Or your family or your friends,
You are in control of yourself and your destiny,
Be the good in society, not the evil
You are you,
And no one can change that.

Max Harrington (13)
Beauchamps High School, Wickford

SIMPLE PAPER

Simple paper,
Why so destructive?
You run the world as if it were your own
You change people
The kindest man becomes selfish when he sees you
The most selfish man becomes the kindest when he loses you
We created each other
Some have a lot of you
Others wish they did
You change people, control lives
So now I ask
Simple paper
Why so destructive?
You run those who created you
Those who you make want more of you
Those who don't have the most of you
So tell me, simple paper
Why do you think this is okay?

Charlie Tye West (12)
Beauchamps High School, Wickford

SELF-HARMING

You're not paper so don't cut it
You're not a book so don't judge it
You're not a coat so don't let the words wear you
Ignore them out so you can shout.

Shout loud, shout proud
Don't let the voices get in your mind
Will anyone stand up for you and be kind?
Each drop of blood is one word falling down.

Love who you are
Don't let bullies harm you
Don't let them think you're not comfortable in your own skin
Think, let it go.

Tasmine Gray (13)
Beauchamps High School, Wickford

THINK

Think about when you drop that litter on the floor.
Think about skipping that homeless person.
Think because that money could change their life.

Life, the thing that brings us together.
Life, without it we wouldn't be here on this Earth.

Earth, the wonderful, amazing place we live on.
Earth, the place life increases and decreases.

Think next time you do something
because your actions have consequences.

Kye Harry Mark Johnson (12)
Beauchamps High School, Wickford

OUR DULL PLANET

Our home, our planet and our only safe keeper,
It holds us safe in its arms and protects us,
We are killing our keeper.

Our only planet, that we are calling home
As we toxify the air
With the black death that consumes the purity of the world.

We create a living Hell on Earth
As we sit back and do nothing about it
Something needs to change.

Jae John Knight (13)
Beauchamps High School, Wickford

DYING QUIETLY

I'm preparing the rods, one, two, three.
Now attaching the bait on Hawk's, waiting for its prey, one,
two, three.
Casting the line out to the abyss, one, two, three.
Hoping that every fisherman's dream will happen and just
waiting for that moment, on and on, one, two, three.
The bell is ringing at the tip of the rod, one two three.
Reeling that fish, fighting with all its might, one, two, three.
Then I see it struggling with human litter around the scaly
body, one, two, three.
I help it and then release it back to sea, one, two, three.
That is my dream just starting, one, two, three.
Now I hope I can inspire others to save the marvellous
creatures dying quietly deep below, one, two, three.
Some don't know what it feels like to be a small, innocent
creature being killed by the actions of a single human being,
one, two, three.
Just remember those who are living like a bee, dying
gradually, one, two, three.
Are we running out of time? One... two...

George Young (12)
Colchester High School, Colchester

THE HUNT

The bark of the hounds, the shout of the men
Run, run, running for my life
Going to reach the river
Hoping the men will call it off.

A hedge, there's a hole in it, perfect
No, a dead end. I'm surrounded, they're everywhere
I can't hold them back
Snarling, growling, teeth are baring.

They're closing in
and the men aren't far behind
But these hounds don't care
I'm done for, my cubs will starve.

My earth is near, I'm so close
Wait, the river, it's there
And there's a gap, run!
Yes, I've made it, I'm in the water.

The hounds, they've given up
I'm safe and alive and my cubs will live
To them, it's a game to rip a fox to shreds
And keep the tail as a trophy.

Oscar Morariu (11)
Colchester High School, Colchester

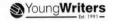

TAKE A STEP INTO REALITY

Let's take a step into reality.
What does everyone see in the world that is so great?
Use your eyes, it's not as perfect as it seems.
It's remorseless and gloomy,
It's delusional and hostile,
It's emotionless and scary.
We walk by people day by day
And some stay to ruin our day tormenting us.
All we ask is for us to forget
These hateful words they say each day.
We can't make them fade away.
Face reality.

The darkness is a hateful demon
It ruins, it takes, it demolishes, it never gives.
Look around you, don't you see? Face reality
What does a perfect world look like?
You see, it has optimism and hilarity
It has light and no hostility.
Face reality.

We know it's not perfect, we wish it could be.
We see a river of blood and we don't bother to care
And all the animals suffer for our health.

You eat them every day,
But don't you see?
You can be as bad as they can be.
If you can't look and see that this isn't right,
Then you don't deserve to eat them all night.
Face reality.

Take a step into a perfect world,
A world where we don't take animals for granted
A world where we appreciate them for themselves, and not
for their meat.
A world where we live in harmony,
Not in endless wars.
Face reality.

Take a step into reality.
We are taken for granted, judged endlessly.
We have to hide ourselves,
You see people covered in make-up,
Covering themselves.
You can accept us for who we are,
And not how we look, speak, act,
Or our religion.
We were never born to be perfect.
We are perfect as we are.
Face reality.

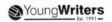

We all have boundless amounts of imperfections
And we can confess them,
Profess them, reveal them, show their stems
And for that, we are condemned.
We can be viewed as ugly,
Terrible, unbearable,
But wouldn't you say we are perfect in a way?
We'd hide our flaws, keep them from the day,
Yet we pay
Because we will say
What flaws, in us, lay.
Face reality.

Take a step into reality.
This is our world!
It's perfect, in a way
We don't have to change
Our perfectly weird world.

Diana Florentina Cocu (12)
Dagenham Park CE School, Dagenham

THE HIDDEN TRUTH

There are life takers at every corner, waiting for victims,
They are thieves stealing lives, not knowing it can't be
undone,
Leaving craters in families' hearts and souls.

As a victim is in the eyes of a life taker, mayhem rises,
Highly trained, vicious guide dogs bark at the sign of knives,
Police officers run into missions, not knowing they could be
their last.

All the people of London hide in their homes,
Hiding in comfort and safety of the brick walls,
As the thieves enter their house. *Bang!*

People dying of cancer all around, hopeless,
Saying their final words with anger and fear,
As the families explode inside out.

All people want is money, all their fancy cars and houses,
As the homeless sit on the streets alone, begging for money
for food,
Dying of hunger as the rich bathe in gold and the poor die.

The world will never be perfect,
We all live with sadness and fear, hoping for something new,
People want much more, what they don't need,
The world will never be perfect and that's what makes it
perfect.

Oliver Zarski (12)
Dagenham Park CE School, Dagenham

A PERFECT DREAM...

The brightness of the stars in
the night sky flooded my mind,
Song singers were away for the night
The furry little creatures gaze at the light
of the moon reflected the shadow of my life.
That dark shadow followed me, chasing me,
Stalking me through the dark corridors
in the haunting school.

Hatred in their heart,
Coldness in their laughter,
Not regretting a moment,
Always causing violence,
Ruling over the learning prison,
Blotches of red cover our arms,
Cuts as deep as the hole in my heart.

My world is perfect,
Perfect in every way.
Well, at least that's what people say.
Face the truth. We all daydream about
smile-spreaders and laugh-makers,
But they don't exist,
Except in a perfect dream.

So pop that bubble,
Stop making it scream
Loud, *loud* in your mind.

But I like to be free,
I like to have my own opinions,
And I wonder about all of those animals,
Floating in the crimson water,
Inhaling the foul stench of death,
And I sometimes think,
Why can't they be free,
Just like us?
Why can't they have their own opinions,
Just like us?
But no.
Cows are whipped, chickens are slit,
Then packaged and sent off, labelled as 'food'.
It didn't have to end up like this,
But it did...

My perfect world,
So imperfect,
Full of imperfections,
yet perfect in every way,
There might be a stabbing here,
A shooting there,
But across the street,
I see a smile as sweet as strawberry jam

Laughter lasting so long,
Sucking all of the air out of your lungs,
Well, at least, that's what people say.

You wish.
Face the truth,
It's all just a perfect dream.
So pop that bubble,
Stop making it scream,
Loud, *loud* in your mind.

Mariah Uddin (11)
Dagenham Park CE School, Dagenham

GOLD CRAVE

There are many conflict makers,
All of the sin stoppers stepped away.
Therefore, there are many fakers,
Then the great clans flocked to them.

On the high street, the big, powerful and rich man sits,
He makes gold the grand gangs.
Then the filth that he spoke drowned the poor in a pit,
They climb, they climb then they stung.

In a world with no harm, love is fluorescent,
A world of peace is a change for friendships.
In a world of empathy, you can feel the pain caused,
With no war, we save our world.

However, in a world of chaos, there is only hope,
So grow some hearts for the poor.
I see you running for the pope,
Just see what you have done.

Quickly, you say no to the idea,
Money. You like it, it is like power, it makes you stronger and evil.
Money! You crave it in London,
Stealing from the dead and orphans on the street.

Danny Payne (12)
Dagenham Park CE School, Dagenham

ANYTHING

I am a man, so powerful and brave
I am a woman and I am treated like a slave
I am a man, stronger than anyone else
I am a woman, weaker than an infant
So what do you see here?
Two genders you can compare
You're wrong by far!
Let's see if this will light a spark
Just tell me anything.

I am healthy, old but free
I have cancer, could you help me, please?
I am healthy just doing sport
I have cancer, I don't want to abort
I am healthy and I change my fate
I have cancer and made mistakes
Cancer? You don't even care
You are human beyond compare
Let's look at a child who everyone cares for
The thing is wouldn't know what to do
Just tell me anything.

I am a child, people care for me
I am an adult, I can work for free
I am a child, I get to learn
I am an adult and I have no concern

I am a child with a big future
I am an adult and I care for nature
Children aren't shoplifters
Adults are good helpers
Poor people don't know how to read
Let's just get them the help they need
Just tell me anything.

I am poor, I need money
I am rich, that doesn't change me
I am poor, I need more sleep
I am rich and that's a huge leap
I am poor, I want help
I am rich, help somebody?
You make my heart melt
I am a human
Feeling there're two worlds
What do we say to a person
Who says there's no reason
For him to exist
Oh I just can't resist
Just tell me anything.

Let's try our best
To pass the test
Not to jump into the pool of death

I need freedom
And so do you
Just tell me anything.

Patrick Kalisz (13)

Dagenham Park CE School, Dagenham

THE CURE

Someone fades away every second, every minute, every
hour...
The number after six. Seven. Seven deadly years. Deadly.
Their desire was to be free,
Not a conflict, crusade or campaign.
Hearts are screaming for a fair democracy!

Now, a seed that has never seen light is gone,
That violent colour is contagious everywhere.
A gullible one knows their end.
Has the dictionary changed?
Our definition of reasonable is a slaughter display!

Our time should not cease before a century!
Neither should there be suffering!
Different flags should stroll casually.
No one treated like property.

Add and subtract,
Eventually, Earth will be a Disney story,
We all know the remedy,
Step out of your category.

Like Heaven and Hell,
Earth has two sides.
Be prepared well,
For this roller-coaster ride.

Zara Shafeeque (13)
Dagenham Park CE School, Dagenham

THE UPSIDE-DOWN WORLD

Life is like a brick wall,
Life is like a Ferris wheel,
Life is about the next Snapchat that you get.
Whatever your life is... live it.
Life is not about bullying or being criticized
For what you like or what you don't.
You could have a passion for Shakespeare
Or how many kills you have on Fortnite.

Bombs, they should be gone,
Fights, they're not a delight.
We all attempt to think like this, but we can't!
The faces at the bus stop are the faces that
mask their stress and anxiety.
You allow the depressing abyss to dissolve your soul,
Rendering you useless.

Slaughter and groans, all can be seen by looking down at
your phone
Blood-drinkers, pig eaters, chicken beaters.
You are a monster.
On your fork is blood, guts, feathers, beaks
and sweet little cheeks.
You are a monster!

A blazing sun reflects on the water.
A gargantuan feast is contained within a basket.
'The winning word from Mum is yet to be heard.
Your adrenaline rushes as you jump in the water,
You shriek and scream as you reach the end of the stream,
Life is like a fairy tale with a peaceful setting but a nasty climax.

The word 'old' is often misused, it is as young as thirty-one or as old as sixty-two.
A grey hair is just there to share your experience.
A pension is just there to show that you've worked hard.
You've lived a good life,
Now it's time to let it go.

What is a perfect world,
Rock bands or poetry slams?
We've had over 2018 years to sort out our world,
So our world is not perfect,
It never will be.

Joseph Dobbins (12)
Dagenham Park CE School, Dagenham

THE UNIVERSE THAT ONLY TAKES OUR TREASURES

This world is nothing but a dream extractor,
Reality is nothing like the X Factor.
In this world, you don't get kicked off a stage,
Deathmakers arrive to take your various, valuable lives in a rage.
Bang! A bullet is shot into your innocent heart,
This is where the pain and agony come to a miserable start.

Racism is hateful and disgusting,
It's the reason why people avoid certain people,
They stay away from certain faces.
Poor, penniless people are lying on dusty streets
How Theresa May strikes the righteous rather than the guilty
How can politics turn out to be so filthy?

Trying to capture that perfect moment,
Sometimes I pity those people in Syria who are helpless,
Their futures depend on those haters,
Those who mourn and cry are the ones who know what the world is really like.

News, media, racism, lies,
It's all you see with those blindfolded eyes,
You don't truly see what the world is like
So when will you open those two naive eyes?
Show Donald Trump, Theresa May and all those other fakers
What the world should be like.

This world will never be perfect,
Always there will be people who are imperfect,
Hate shall become remarkably contagious,
I know that this might sound outrageous,
However, this is the truth,
You do not even have to search for proof!

Are we always to see life takers?
Are we to see hate makers?
Are we to see death lovers?
Are we to see our own deaths arrive?
If this is what the real world is like
Then I cannot even imagine what a perfect world would be
like!

Zareen Ahmed (11)
Dagenham Park CE School, Dagenham

AN IMPERFECT WORLD

Isn't the world a beautiful place?
A wonderful utopia of infinite grace,
Blessed with the miracle of life,
Freed from strife,
Hang on a second...

An ominous darkness pollutes the skies,
The tragic death of Mother Nature!
And yet people believe one man's lies
"Nonsense! Global warming is a hoax!"
"It's cold outside!"
Sound familiar?

Monolithic towers lost in a sea of isolation,
Eyes transfixed on another dimension,
Divided forever, closer than ever,
In a world where light is the key to darkness.

Your sex dictates your prominence,
dominance and relevance,
While beliefs and skin dictate your status.
A man can be as controversial as he likes,
But a woman speaks out and is chained to the
omnipotent walls of our society.

The world is a diverse dwelling,
Filled with luscious trees, canopies of leaves
And brilliant shades of emerald-green,
Generating life for you and me.
People of all styles, like foods in an aisle.

Some love the agony and sorrow of others,
Others rally, assisting others in need,
Supporting them to succeed,
The opposite of greed.

Many politicians are like the former,
Exploitation, deportation, incrimination
In their morals and in their pride
And they absquatulate when condemned.

"Tyranny!" they cried in the middle ages
"And such is life!" we reply in the 21st century.

Ethan-Scott Hin (13)
Dagenham Park CE School, Dagenham

THE IMPERFECT WORLD

So many innocent people getting killed,
Others just take pills,
Can't bear to live in a world of war,
The Lord's destiny was not fulfilled.

The world is a cruel place,
An inconsistent, inequitable, inimical ecosystem of pain and
suffering.
But seeking peace makes me seem like a hopeless dream
chaser,
The war in Syria is worse than a disgrace,
A daughter will die before her mother manages to embrace.

Infant mortality is intensifying, increasing, heightening
But nobody even cares that all these innocent kids are dying
No police, no sirens,
We've constantly got bombs disrupting the silence.

Wait a minute...
It couldn't be any clearer,
We're the ones who caused this pollution and global
warming,
And we're getting nearer and nearer to the polar bear's
extinction,
The ice is melting, all the animals are sinking.

It's our fault,
Only a few people have made a distinction.

I'm tired of police brutality
Whatever happened to society?
Young black kids
Getting attacked for the stuff they never did
And now they're all suffering from anxiety.

In my perfect world, there would be no disease,
No pharmacies,
You could walk around the streets with ease,
There would be no police,
'Cause there would be no one to cease,
Everyone would live in a world of peace.

D'Khaari Marquis Changlee (13)
Dagenham Park CE School, Dagenham

TRUE JUSTICE!

Inequality, disparity, preferentiality, irregularity
We live in a world with so much barbarity
Where people judge you for your peculiarity
Due to these views, we're blocked from prosperity
Our lives are clouded with no shred of sincerity
True justice!

Politics, policies, negative economies
We live in a world controlled by a sly puppeteer
Brainwashed and hypnotised by the sin whisperer.
Distracted by the booms and flames engulfing Syria
On our money-draining streets, poverty scars a girl named
Delia
True justice!

Extinguished, vanished, vanquished, deceased
We live in a world where the white rhino has its days
numbered
While in our ignorance we eat, envy, excite and slumber
Donald calls global warming 'fake news'
The polar bears are suffering, battered and bruised
True justice!

Terrorism, sexism, extremism, racism
These views are nothing but country demolishers
These knights of treachery, these evil accomplishers

Over half a million people have been killed in Syria
The people are treated as though they are bacteria
True justice!

Corrupted justice is the root of our mistake
True justice! is the light out of this hollow snake
Our lives should be just as sweet as Miranda
Join me, to a perfect world like Wakanda
Our perfect world, true justice!

Kehinde Ajayi (13)
Dagenham Park CE School, Dagenham

IS IT REAL?

The river of hate will sweep you away,
It smells of blood and violence...
The dark, devilish water will transform your thoughts to war
and corruption!
The further down the river you go, the more restless it gets!
Why should I keep this monstrosity in my perfect world?
Why should I?

The river of hate has a twin,
It is as transparent as glass and as peaceful as a newborn
baby!
This river is called love...
You would slowly go down the heart-warming and never-
ending river.
Why should I keep this in my perfect world?
Because it is the key to my world.

A knot that can't be broken!
Yet people try to cut it open.
The evil in it will leave you, desert you,
Stay and it will hurt you.
Hate builds it up...
Envy sucks!

This knot is so tight it can never be undone.
People call it friendship.
It is as if a hand were grasping on to you...

Usually, there would be clouds in my head,
But you would push them all away!
Peace is an ideal that we all want,
It is what Martin Luther King Jr. spoke about.
All pain and wars are stopped by this barrier!
This is my perfect world, are you in it?

War is not needed,
It is filled with arrogance and stupidity!
Yet people agree to build it up!
This will never be my perfect world!

Nathaniel George Joseph Davis (12)
Dagenham Park CE School, Dagenham

WE'RE DOOMED

Our generation won't be known for anything.
Never will anybody say we were the peak of mankind.
That isn't wrong. The truth is, our generation was a failure.
Thinking that we actually succeeded was a waste.
We think living only for money and power is the way to go.
Being loving, helpful, respectful, kind are stupid things to do.
Forgetting about that time will not be easy but we will try.
Changing our world for the better is something we never did.
Giving up was how we handled out problems
Working hard was a joke.
We knew that people thought we couldn't come back.
That might be true unless we turn things around.

Unless we turn things around that might be true.
People thought we couldn't come back.
We knew that was a joke.
Working hard was how we handled our problems.
Giving up is something we never did.
Changing our world for the better won't be easy but we'll try.
Forgetting about that time is a stupid thing to do.
Being loving, helpful, respectful and kind is the way to go.
Living only for money and power is a waste.
And we think we actually succeeded.
Thinking that our generation was a failure.

That is wrong, the truth is, we were the peak of mankind. Never will anybody say our generation isn't known for anything.

Jenson Jay Hattam (12)

Dagenham Park CE School, Dagenham

MY PERFECT WORLD WOULD BE...

My perfect world would be...
A world with no negativity,
No one living in poverty,
Keeping all the same diversity,
Everyone having equal opportunities,
To see what their life is really meant to be.

My perfect world would be...
Neutral,
Everyone would be mutual,
Everything would be useful,
Not using too much, no we can't be so cruel.

It wouldn't be where people steal for a meal,
Stealing for a feeling,
Ticking time bombs in their heads,
Can't remember the days.
Just before they're dead,
Spinning like a merry-go-round,
At a fairground, seeing the gangs,
Then the blackout.

A small dog,
Beautiful, natural, wild and free,
Yet it's not always friendly.

It bites and scares,
The blood-curdling scare of big bears
Leaves scars.
Every ounce of sweat trickling off their head,
Then they say, "Ta ta!"

The world can be dark,
The realm of mankind can be tough.
Our minds detect our surroundings,
And turns them into emotions.
Hear the crashing of the oceans.
Wake up with the sound of a dog's bark.

A beautiful beach at sunset,
Where we should meet,
This would be the perfect world for me.

Madison Bostock (13)
Dagenham Park CE School, Dagenham

PROUD TO BE HUMAN (SOMETIMES)

We start in Syria.
The ash-engulfed skies are the embedded marks of war.
Will Assad embark on his homicides again, who's to know for sure?
We Brits are scared to intervene,
Our morals are messed up.
"Oh look, Russians! Should we turn back, sir?"
As a scaredy-cat would say: "Yup!"

Slavery was abolished years ago, you say?
Get your facts corrected,
It's happening in Libya today.
The torture and suffering we can only sympathise with.
Ultimately, slavery should have been dealt with forthwith.

Despite these flaws in our present day,
By the seas and sky is my breath stolen away.
The Himalayas tower astoundingly over surrounding countries,
God's creation is everything,
From the deep black of space to your aunties!

What would the world be like without God's mercifulness,
But a barren wasteland with tumbleweeds in the wilderness?

I see the rosy-red of my mother's love,
Spread swiftly around like a flock of doves.

Analyse the details and you will discover,
That in all inches of the earth, love calmly hovers,
This imperfect world of ours is perfect in some cases,
For instance, look upon most of us and you will see happy
faces.

Danyaal Abdul-Bateen Mukit (13)
Dagenham Park CE School, Dagenham

LIFE'S WAY

Every day, everywhere
Today's society is just not fair
In daylight or at night
Every turn I take there's a constantly a fight
Life is not always going to be friends with you
He will stab you in the back and show that he's not true.

People out there feeling worthless and heartbroken
Yet we don't have a minute to spare to help those in despair
but we don't care about the current affairs
We need to help those in need and stop being money-
blinded.
Nevertheless we just don't give a-

But let's move the dark clouds aside
And bring the radiant sunshine into our lives
Show a smile to lighten up someone's day
Who knows, you might wash their misery away.

There's always light; a glimmer of hope
To show that, maybe, this life is not just a slippery slope
If we slip and plunge down to the bottom
We must build our way to the top, to allow our true desires
to blossom.

This world will continuously be a confusing place
They say that positives outweigh negatives, well that's not
the case

There will never be a perfect world that exists in this universe,
This is a jail you can't escape, we are stuck just like prisoners.

Mariyum Yatoo (13)
Dagenham Park CE School, Dagenham

OUR SOCIETY

The world is perfect and imperfect,
If you're able, you'll surf it.
Those conflict-makers,
Are the real devastators.
So don't blame yourself,
We will need your help.

A blissful world,
Will be full of boys and girls.
No theft, no crime,
You will have all the time.
Just a dozen hours for your work,
And a few hours to halt criminals who lurk.

But in our society today,
There are only small bursting rays.
Why do they commit crimes?
They don't have the right to kill others, then die.
Those precious minutes of your life that remain,
Might just have the most pain.

So what is wrong with society?
The people are trembling with anxiety,
What is wrong? Can't we all get along?

Everyone gather round, let's have a sing-song,
I know it's not that easy,
But we have to start somewhere, cleaning all that graffiti.

The world is perfect and imperfect,
Are you able to surf it?
The peace-makers
Are trying their best to save us
We are still fighting the battle. *Boom!*
Will you be a chicken and run? *Zoom!*
The world is perfect and imperfect.

Isaac Angbore (11)
Dagenham Park CE School, Dagenham

MYTHICAL WORLD

For racism and human ignorance, I am almost in despair,
For racism is around me, everywhere,
So many people are judged by their race,
This is the world, which is a disgrace.

Stupid teenagers roam around the streets,
Looking around for targets to meet.
Though we live in a so-called democracy,
Of racism, we will never be free.

Violence,
Terrorists bombing places everywhere,
Spreading and infecting minds like bacteria,
People criticise the fights for women's rights,
Unknowing of what they face in their lives.

Paradise,
This world isn't a paradise,
It had its own ups and downs,
This isn't the end,
It is just a beginning,
So let's join and say, "End racism!"

Life is a continuous cycle of hate,
That we can't negate

Yet our own leaders can't even translate
The fact that there are problems in this world
That we just can't ignore.
It's the green light that blinds their eyes,
Blurring out the truth,
Corrupting us with lies.

A perfect world is a myth,
Everything you've worked for won't always be achieved.

Taiwo Ajayi (13)
Dagenham Park CE School, Dagenham

EARTH

War, war, war
But after that, we will close the door
To the poor, do they deserve more?
Perhaps we should shed some light
On the war in Syria: a seven-year fight
Maybe we should think about
Men, women and children engulfed in flames
Instead of our own country's aims.

Diseases, diseases everywhere
Minuscule particles
Floating in the air
But do they really care?
You may not notice that death is a soul stealer
You had better watch out for that drug dealer.

US boasting about their achievements
Like bombing IS
How about a peace agreement?

The perfect world is one without crime
Helping starving children in Ethiopia
A race against time
No poverty
No disease
No hunger

God, help us all if you please
Help us all, do not let us fall
Help us stand tall and knock down the walls.

No racism, nor sexism
No need to jump into that endless chasm
Of lies and despair.

If we had this, we should be glad
That in our world there is no bad
But I guess this world will just have to do
But anyone can change the world, including you.

Jailen Stainsbury (13)
Dagenham Park CE School, Dagenham

PEOPLE

On a small planet called Earth
In the solar system
Once a peaceful planet
Now corrupted by anger.
Stated as a place of joy
Now misery all over.
Following rules of Mother Nature
Now abusing intelligence to demolish it.
Once harmonious, in full glory
The need for conflict all of a sudden.

Now coming to an end
Air polluted
Oceans contaminated
Animals extinct.
The air I breathe today may also be the last.
The dry lips I now have
May never again feel a fresh taste.
The only friend I ever had
Is the last one of our kind
And the empathy for his family
May leave me in depression for centuries.

Economy collapsing
Education is shot
Police are corrupted.

Everything in society is broken
Intelligence is shunned
Ignorance is rewarded.
People are depressed and angry
We can't live with each other
And can't live with ourselves.
We pass each other
If we do interact
It's meaningless robotic communication.
People want fifteen seconds of fame
Rather than a lifetime of meaning and purpose.
Because we are corrupt.

Rokas Vaikasas (12)
Dagenham Park CE School, Dagenham

SHE THOUGHT SHE WAS PERFECT

Inside she's crying, outside she's smiling,
Her heart has been crushed and casually thrown away,
She's struggling to cope with each passing day,
It's been months since her mum was taken away.

She remembers that day when she walked through the park
a spectacular way,
She remembers that day when she sang in the rain,
Happiness and excitement, and now shame,
The love that she shared you can never deny,
Just thinking about it leads her to cry.

Her love was like a beautiful wave,
I know she'd do anything to make it stay
But was it meant to reach its end?
Was it meant to reach its shore?

She suffered much in silence,
Her spirit did not bend,
She faced her pain with courage,
Until the very end.

Her life was full of loving deeds,
Forever thoughtful of her special needs,
Today and tomorrow, their whole lives through,
They will love and believe in you.

If she could see her one last time,
I know what she'd do
Release all her emotions
And say, "Mum, I love you."

I know how it feels because my precious one died too.

Aaliyah Nassor (12)
Dagenham Park CE School, Dagenham

BEING

I bet we all heard about *being* before,
One way or another,
Well-being, being and other beings,
Let me tell you about them all.

In our big, bustling, busy world,
They hoard us as their food,
For society is a nuke aimed at a single person!
In addition, that single person is us.

We live in a world where no one cares about anything,
Well... except money.
The sad, lonely, excluded
Cannot be heard here.

There is not a way to get out of this hole
As it digs itself to bury more victims.
Social media shovelling the muddy, dirty lies,
Then posing, acting as dolls.

So let us not be like paper,
For it's swayed by the intimidating winds.
Let us be instead free birds,
For they can fly anywhere.

However, I will not lie,
The world has its good sides

For we care about each other
And, just a bit,
About things that matter.

For I see the fact is dawning that, should we be vile,
Consequences are unbearable
And foes impeccable
Will fall on us as snowflakes,
Yet as deadly as assault rifles.

Amal Mathew Kuriakose (14)
Dagenham Park CE School, Dagenham

I DREAM

The world is big,
Full of people,
Some are good,
But some are bad.

Gangs roam the streets,
I ask myself, "What is it they need?"
I see guns being loaded,
Bang! I hear when they have exploded,
People are looking high,
Because the drugs have taken over their minds.

I dream that the world be free of gangs,
No more people afraid of them,
No more guns exploding,
No more guns being loaded,
People in control of their minds,
Because they've won their fights.

But you come back to the real world.
And see the reality,
You see wars and fighting,
You see people killing,
You see people crying,
But you don't help them,
Because you can't.

I dream every day,
That all countries at war are free,
That nobody will be crying on the floor,
That everyone will fly,
And make the most of their lives

And I still dream of girls being treated equally,
I dream of there being no inequality,
For every day I fight and fight,
Just so I can see the light.

Nour Khalfaoui (11)
Dagenham Park CE School, Dagenham

MY DREAM WORLD IS A PLACE WITH UPS AND DOWNS

My world is a place without crime
Murder, poverty and anything bad are myths
There is no time there, which means there is no rush
So sit back, relax and hush.
Sometimes I am in the park until it's dark
Or in the pool where it's cool
But everywhere, yes everywhere, is filled with dread
As the floor is covered in red
Gangs are in there, where they wait for someone to scare.
The world can be cruel or nice, like a...
Hate maker
Love giver
Bee stinger
Health bringer
But this is my world, a place with possibilities
With lots of positivity
But the world can be a crushing wave of defeat
You don't know where to go
Feel like you have taken a blow
And through all this, you want to start over again

You forget something really important:
Your purpose in life!
So be filled with strife
Through all your problems
'Cause this is a beginning not an end
But sometimes you need a friend.

Vincent Osazee Johnson (11)
Dagenham Park CE School, Dagenham

MY PERFECTLY IMPERFECT WORLD

Although it might not be perfect
It might seem a little bit wrecked
I still love my world
My perfectly imperfect world.

Life-taker
Fear-creator
People-hater
Fly-eater
Web-maker
Out of all the insects
I'm the best
What am I?
Have you guessed?
Of course you know
I am a spider!

In a perfect world
There are no slugs and snails stealing left and right
There will only be butterflies and ladybugs
Giving to the poor.

In the perfect world
There is no war
Bang! A bomb just hit my door
It was as loud as a blaring horn
That's my perfectly imperfect world.

In a perfect world
There will be no injustice
All peace.

Although that sounds fun
It sounds quite boring
Unlike my perfectly imperfect world
Which is fun, crazy and perfectly imperfect.

In the end, I am proud
Proud of my world
My perfectly imperfect world.

Maria Anuoluwapo Odusina (11)
Dagenham Park CE School, Dagenham

UNWANTED REALITY

What is your perfect world?
Mine has no hate, no sorrow, no pain,
It has love, happiness and no dying in vain.
There is no death,
And no one draws their final breath.

There is no icy laughter,
No lashes of pain,
Nobody is afraid.
But what am I afraid of?
Is it the crows that parade?

Beneath my world,
What is there?
All the bad is locked up,
So there is no reason to be sad.

In reality, children are still
As they become paralysed with fear.
A single tear,
Lost in torn places.
A lot of faces...

A block of sadness,
Placed to help somebody suffocate...

Death-causers,
Pain-bringers,
Void-makers.
We are human,
Yet treated as the gods of the valley.

A cloud of sadness hangs over us.
The tears of the world,
I've never known,
Until now.
Peacemakers,
Comfort-bringers,
Humans can be good if they try.

Rugile Zarankaite (12)
Dagenham Park CE School, Dagenham

PERFECT WORLD

I see a world un-plagued by humanity,
A landscape with a sense of sanity.
Trees stand proud.
Life finally makes a crowd.
We should never have been around.

In the fall of man,
The sky blots out.
Shooting stars are tongues of flame.
Oceans writhe.
Mythology thrives.

This world, here and now,
Where we dwell,
Could do without rumours,
As they spread like tumours.
All they are,
Are simple sparks,
But we all know sparks can burn like wildfire.

If Mother Nature must watch us grow,
Why must the military, police and firefighters
Risk their lives,
For a sliver of money,
That we earn behind a desk.

Why does this world
Suffer under the likes of Trump?
Why do the leaders
Often end up the betrayers?

If we must live
In my perfect world,
Let not the rich take from the poor,
But give to them,
For we really are all equal.

Andrew Frederick Böenke (12)
Dagenham Park CE School, Dagenham

THOSE FAKERS

Intoxicated and oblivious,
Fake people dominate the playground,
Waiting for their next prey,
Those fakers.

You feel isolated, trapped,
But they're your only friends,
We all feel in our hearts that we have to let them go
somehow,
Yet you don't have the power to do so,
Those fakers.

They'll take everything,
Leave you with nothing,
Laugh at you falling,
Into a dark pit,
They'll leave you,
Those fakers.

The pain will finally start to sink in,
Dragging you into your mistakes,
Your tears will make your own ocean,
Sinking deep underwater,
Shattering you into pieces that can never be fixed,
Those fakers.

Intoxicated and oblivious,
Fake people dominate the playground,
Waiting for their next prey...
I was victimised,
Those fakers.

Arselma Beth Sam (11)
Dagenham Park CE School, Dagenham

PERFECT/IMPERFECT WORLD POEM

In my perfect world,
Everyone will live forever.
No one will be a soul taker,
Or ever need to arrange low-spirited parties.

In my perfect world,
No one will ever be sick.
No one will need to become a sickness healer,
Or ever take a get well potion.

In my perfect world,
All you can smell are amazing foods and fragrances.
There will be no disgusting, dreadful, stinky cheese,
Or gossiping of rotten people.

In my perfect world,
Everyone will be safe.
No one will think of having battles,
Or being a life ended.

In my perfect world,
Everyone's life is like a jewel.
Our lives are very valuable,
Let others appreciate it too.

In my perfect world,
Everyone is outstanding.
In their own special ways,
Don't you think? I do.

Jennifer Goncalves (12)
Dagenham Park CE School, Dagenham

THE 'AMAZING' WORLD

They say the world is 'amazing',
But to me,
It seems like it's always changing.
From politics to equality,
From attacks to education.

What is this great world that seems to be?

If the world is as great as it seems to be,
Then why is there pollution in the sea?

People like you and me,
Did this you see,
But not everyone gets chance to plead
For clean water, food, shelter, happiness
And enough jobs for you and me.

People across the world suffer from diseases,
Homelessness and starvation
But what are you and I doing
To help those in need?
An 'amazing' world you see!

School shootings
Gun crimes, threats
Poachers and extinction
But what do you and I do?
An 'amazing' world you see!

Elikya Manata (12)
Dagenham Park CE School, Dagenham

PERFECT WORLD

When I take a walk outside at night,
When the world has gone to sleep,
You can hear the wind sings different tunes,
To the ones you normally hear,
But it's choking on the words we are too afraid to hear.

We live in a world where we only live to die,
In a place where people just want to run and hide,
People fake smiles so people don't know what's inside,
Others wish they could just go back in time.

I always look up to the sky,
Thinking about a perfect world,
A world where no tears, fears or darkness are found,
No crime to pay,
Black, yellow, white or red would laugh and sing,
Smiles and waves would exist,
In my perfect world, mankind would be kind,
This is what happens when I take a walk outside at night.

Goda Petraviciute (12)
Dagenham Park CE School, Dagenham

A PERFECT WORLD

When I was growing up there was terrorism,
Everywhere I wasn't accepted.
The air was filled with pollution, poverty and crime - crime.
The bullies gave me a shock to, my head, my skull.

But beauty came from above,
It was like a signal of love,
Peace, together like one, together like one!

It was all great, great again,
No wars, no *more!*
No crime, no *more!*
So perfect, so wonderful, no one could perceive it!

My perception was so confused!
But then it all became clear...

It was all great, great again,
No wars, no more!
No crime, no more!
So perfect, so wonderful,
No one could perceive it, perceive it!

Well, it was perfect.

William Brian Matthews (12)
Dagenham Park CE School, Dagenham

MY HOME COUNTRY

My heart was beating like a wildfire,
Everything was a blur,
My whole life was a desire,
Now it was getting packed into a car.

The dust in my eyes,
The spices in my mouth,
How the love of my country stabs,
Hurts and makes me froth.

My life was changing to a dry cloth,
As I start my life again with nothing but loss,
I was flung away like a moth,
Far, far away from the laughter and floss.

The sound of the water crashing course,
Never needing to leave its home,
I want to live my life with such force,
But I was feeling like vaporised foam.

Mother says, "Ready to wander?"
I say, "No, just wonder."

Juwariyah Zubair (12)
Dagenham Park CE School, Dagenham

NON-VIOLENT TO DEMOLITION

The world used to be peaceful
Flowers used to bloom
Optimistic colours would bloom.

Birds hummed the song
Nature's song was heard everywhere
The greenery was vivid.

My mother was there until this happened...

The destruction of the greenery was gone
No more to see that was peace
I wish this didn't happen

Factories were built
Only a little bit of greenery was left
This thing was harmful to the mother.

Was this supposed to happen?

There are only some lands which have greenery
where's my happiness gone?

I am Mother Nature
Nobody ruins my happiness!

Ritthyha Kumanan (12)
Dagenham Park CE School, Dagenham

IMAGINE...

Imagine being able to walk not in fear
Not being scared of the unknown coming near
Imagine not having to hear about hardship happening here
and there
Imagine if innocent lives weren't crushed by explosives
Neglected and deprived, no food or water to survive
Left there to die, living a lonely life
Being told a bitter lie, obeying the government, nowhere to
hide
A word out of your mouth and you won't leave alive
Strained, no way to strive
Being set somewhere you won't survive
Imagine life with sweetness and joy
Love and affection
Hope and success
And nothing less
Imagine moments to treasure
Not living under pressure
Imagine...

Chanel Kyel (13)
Dagenham Park CE School, Dagenham

WHEN THE WORLD IS ASLEEP, I STAY AWAKE

When the world is asleep, I stay awake,
I hear nothing but owls,
And cars going around.

When the world is asleep, I stay awake,
I hear many fights,
But do nothing but stare at the moonlight.

When the world is asleep, I stay awake,
Thinking very deep until it turns late,
When the world is asleep, I stay awake,
Not a soul in sight, except mine.

When the world is asleep, I stay awake,
The wind blows the trees, the only life in sight is me,
When the world is asleep, I stay awake,
I hear a single heartbeat throughout my day.

When the world is asleep, I stay awake,
Life is not there when the world is asleep.

Tanisha Zaman (12)
Dagenham Park CE School, Dagenham

THE VIOLENCE FROM GANGS

Cruel masked men looking innocent
Looking for the innocent to be dead
As if it is a death cycle that never stops.

Floating knives coming closer
Heart beating quickly
Blood pumping, gasping for air
Suffocating, and blood is on your side.

Anonymous people ready to run
Ready to run as if a black, gloomy cloud
Was going to gobble them up
And take them away.

Parents and sulky siblings
Missing the innocent people they loved
Life-changing moments always occur.

Unless the anchor is dropped
This makes the lonely family feel a tragic life ahead
Drip, drop, making the raging river larger.

Daeem Zaki (12)
Dagenham Park CE School, Dagenham

THE WORLD WHERE GOOD THINGS OVERCOME BAD THINGS

The world of perfect imperfections,
The world of life and death.
The world of happiness and sadness,
The world where good things overcome bad things.

Racism is a creature of ignorance that people use to hurt,
The cloud of smoke drifts.
Beside the long, isolated roads of loneliness,
Like a thread from a spider's web.

Bullying is an act people take a lot of,
It's cruelty itself.
The cruelty of bullying sails,
Like a ship sailing towards me.

Happiness is a smile, it's laughter, it's love,
It's the joy of dreams.
Above my world of love,
Like a velvet ribbon lying on my head.

Carlota Jesus (12)
Dagenham Park CE School, Dagenham

MAKE A DIFFERENCE!

Do the right thing, make a difference
Let your mind figure out our world
This world
The one that's full of failure, darkness and disgrace...

Do the right thing, make a difference
Change our world to a better one
Yes, this world
Make this world peaceful, happy and everlasting...

Do the right thing, make a difference!
Change this world to your perfection
Once again, this world,
Transform this world to have equality and respect...

I was once told that this is my world and I must change it
before someone else does...

Do the right thing, make a difference!

Kaneez Fatima (12)
Dagenham Park CE School, Dagenham

I AM...

I am the emptiness you feel at 5am,
I am the tears with no meaning and the pain when you smile,
I am the scar that covers your body and pushes away your closest friends,
I am the voice you despise but will soon learn to trust,
I am the demon that screams keeping you up all the time,
I am the only thing that comes along when you awaken in the morning,
I am the one and only thing you will feel...

Rebekah Hughes (12)
Dagenham Park CE School, Dagenham

WARNING

I don't care if you're six or twenty-three,
This right here will change the way you think about life.
If you don't drop everything and listen to me,
Your days will be filled with pain and strife.

I'm sorry if I ruin every kid's dream,
I know it's not my place to tell an adult how to do their job,
But at the end of a tunnel, there's a beam,
And because of that beam, your childhood and freedom will
be robbed.

How do I put this in a way kids will understand?
Being a teen is not fantastic.
You think it's all parties and that everything's grand,
But if I'm honest, the stories are one hundred percent
plastic.

Don't run away from my words, parents,
This will affect you too.
If you ever tell a teen that you understand,
Just know that we can tell when you lie
Because you still punish us anyway.

If you have listened to my point of view
Things will go better for you in life.
Just remember that being a teen is the hardest.
Don't put pressure on us.
I'm warning you.

Cara Graca Chapatarongo (13)
Grays Convent High School, Grays

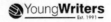

YOU CAN STOP THIS

Don't lie
When you say you love me
I know you don't.

Don't lie
When you say I matter
The world says different

Don't lie
When you say that the cuts that decorate me
don't need to happen
Because they do.

Don't lie
When you say I exist
You have never seen the real me.

Don't lie
When you say I'm accepted
My mum begs to differ

Don't lie
When you say you care
You didn't stop this from happening

Don't lie
When you say I'm needed
I'm a waste of space

Don't lie
When you say I'm fearless
I'm scared

Don't lie
When you say you notice me
You never see the pain

Don't lie
When you say I'm pretty
You only see the make-up.

Don't lie
Never lie
Because these lies do not benefit me
Especially because
I'm dead.

I woke up every morning
tears dried on my face
I washed my face clean
Leaving no trace.

Walking to school
Wincing in every step
No one seemed to care
Since the shadows is where I'm kept

Punch after punch
Kick after kick

I only ate a crumb
But now I'm going to be sick

Was now the end?
I couldn't take anymore
Look out the window, there's Death
Knocking at my front door

I open my wide door
But when he entered I went stiff
Not bothering you anymore
Now I lay among the cliff

How could you stop this horrid deed?
Everyone needs to know
Losing people is not what we need
People leaving as cold as snow

Saving people today and tomorrow
Telling them to reflect
Only then will death be lifted with sorrow
People are all imperfect

Being the one to stop it all
Understanding every feeling
Loving everyone as they are
Living with no hate
You are the one who can stop the fall

In all, be life's meaning
Not all go as far
Go now before it's too late!

Sara Ahmed (13)
Grays Convent High School, Grays

THE BALLAD OF THE TIME WITHIN LONDON

One day we went up to London
Train tickets in our hands
We wanted to explore the kingdom
That controlled most of the land

We walked up to Big Ben
We ambled across Tower Bridge
We went to see the red marching men
We saw an ice rink colder than a fridge

Then we stopped off for some lunch
In London, any restaurant will fit your mood
Out of our pizzas, we took a big munch
What an utterly wonderful array of food

And for dessert, we had mouth-watering ice cream
Melting rapidly in its cones
It was an absolute dream
better than a day glued to your phone.

See how fun London once was?
And now it is coated with terror and crime
And if children ask parents why the answer is just 'because'
All of this is as sour as a ripe lime.

I wish this would change forever
No more jeopardising people's health
So we can be in unity together
Like one thousand bees in a hive.

Now people are afraid of leaving their houses
This should not happen in a world full of humans
Why are we made to feel as scared as a mouse?
Is this what is brought about by man?

So much misery comes in rain showers
Red tears stain the cobbled road
None of these bringing flowers
London is in worry mode

But in the future happiness will come
And we can still enjoy the ride on the trains
And run around freely with our dads and mums
And there would be no need to complain

For we would run around carefree
In happiness and glee.

Siân Kira Arkan (13)
Grays Convent High School, Grays

MEMORIES: THE DAGGERS

The sweat dripped off your forehead,
the forehead encasing sins,
It tasted oh-so bitter yet ever so sweet.
My sea-like tears fused with my blood,
I remembered the day we met.
The sun was glaring down, reflecting off your face,
Your eyes, perfectly pretty, gazed in amazement at the
sunset that lay before you.
Your hair, like a current, flowed with no care,
neither of us knew.

You were the one to cause me the most pain,
Your smell, your laughter, your actions, your ways.
The screaming that convinced me that
any other place was better than this,
The screaming that tempted me to end my days.
Love was the sunbeam piercing my window,
Memories, the daggers piercing my heart.
Your smile, the smile that consumed all of my being,
But now, at least we can finally be apart.

Your figure in my mind when I close my eyes
Not the you that I met on that day
But the you that shadowed over me,
stripping me of my dignity.

You took every part of me that you could
and still, I would not stay away.
You had me on your line,
winding me in whenever you needed me,
Then casting me out when you had had enough.
"I am a person!" I screamed, determined yet dreadful,
Hoping that those words would not put me in the rough.

Did you ever say, 'I love you'?
Did you say it in sun or thunder?
When you apologised for being with another,
Or when I was smothering you and drowning you
Deep in the water?

Jodie Rae Fullerton (13)
Grays Convent High School, Grays

THE DOOR TO THE FUTURE

The door is there, the door will always be there,
But I'm too afraid to go near.
I'm too afraid to go up to the door,
to hold its frame and look down.
Because I know what I'll see,
I'll see the world below me,
A world that I'm not ready to jump into.

I never go to the door
but I go to the window and look straight ahead.
The coward's way out.
And here I know I'm safe without a doubt
Because here by the window,
if I lean forward, I will press myself against the glass,
But if I lean out of the door
I will fall and watch years of my life pass.

I'm not ready to face the future,
I'm clueless and unprepared,
I'll get swallowed up by an army of clocks that'll limit my life
And of that, I'm scared.
So here I stay, away from the door,

Choosing between being stuck in the present
or facing the future
And, if I'm honest, I don't know which scares me more.

Amreet Dhillon (13)
Grays Convent High School, Grays

MUSIC TO MY HEART

First day of school, I was drawn to your flute
The blissful melody flooded my ears
The symphony echoed then became mute
Time then sped up, have I known you for years?

I'm addicted to your cinnamon scent
I want to touch hands in the popcorn cup
You are my prince, I ask your consent
Let's go on a date, I'll wear my make-up.

Life is not a movie, there are no retakes
There's only one chance, let's make it worthwhile
With you in the frame, my life's a cupcake
Savoury and snappy, sweet and smiles.

Chasing after you has made me weary
But I've caught you now so don't get teary.

Jessica Westell (13)
Grays Convent High School, Grays

SINGLE-SIDED LOVE

My love for you - too painful to express,
because you know how much I love you.
You turn away to make me love you less,
It doesn't work as my love is not new.

You know that my love is everlasting,
You cannot fool me, even when you try.
You do not like love, as you fear it passing,
Cloud your mind and heart as you sit and cry.

You say, "But we have been friends for years,"
That love between us would never work out.
And once it is said, I shed a few tears,
I need to hold in the urge to shout.

My love for you - too painful to express,
Because you hate me, I must love you less.

Abigail Cosgrave (13)
Grays Convent High School, Grays

MYSTERIOUS LOVE

What is love, where is love, why is love here?
Can it be caught or is it created?
Is it the feeling when food is near?
Is this feeling accepted or hated?

Can love be sealed up, wrapped up and gifted?
Because there are many I would give it to.
They would smile, their low spirits lifted,
Others need it to know that it's true.

Love is invisible, love's in the air,
In fact, love's probably in me and you,
Or even love could be lurking in here,
Glaring at the victim, could it be you?

Love's a mystery that no one can solve,
But we don't need answers, we already knew!

Sanna Hashimi (13)
Grays Convent High School, Grays

PICTURE-PERFECT FANTASY

Why do your eyes turn away from my gaze?
Where lies the beauty in each other's mind?
Your perfect eyes are always amazing,
Your healing touch is one of a kind.

Do you believe in a soulmate?
Nowadays, love comes in all shapes and all sizes,
Could sparks fly on just the first date?
Only the winner takes home the first prize.

All the heads turn when you walk into the room,
I would silence the stars if you asked so,
When all is sadness, you lift up the gloom,
I love you so much that you'll never know.

I know our love may be complicated,
But baby, our love is underrated.

Niamh White (13)
Grays Convent High School, Grays

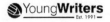

HEARTBREAK

One broken bond, two broken hearts,
That's what happens when love takes charge.
Things are shattered, left in parts,
Things unspoken becoming too large.

Three magic words that make four eyes dull,
Shiny droplets form in their eyes.
Not even their parents can help to console,
Where there was love, there now is despise.

Four days later, three new words are spoken,
They are now strong, they are like new.
Formed by a heart which has just been broken,
These three words are: I'm over you.

Lily Rebekah Knights (13)
Grays Convent High School, Grays

RED, ORANGE, GREEN... GO!

The truth is meant to help people, not hurt
How do you stop yourself from reaching the edge?
Stay alert! What if it's too late?
I dare you to tell the truth.

When the light turns green, get ready to fade away
Don't worry, it's too late for you to stay
It will all be over in a matter of seconds
I dare you to tell the truth.

It's me or you, this is the end
Your heart is mine to lend
Truth or dare?
Let the games begin.

Aida Mataj (13)
Grays Convent High School, Grays

JUST FOR YOU

You stare at me with your blue eyes
Your fingers holding my hand
That stare of yours makes me sigh
You act like my biggest fan.

This is for your ears only
Your eyes as well
You comfort me when I am lonely
You're the one, I can tell.

You run and play
You I would never doubt
I would sit with you all day
Because I love all you're about.

We would die for each other
You're the best little brother.

Niamh Dennis (12)
Grays Convent High School, Grays

LOST CONSTELLATIONS

A formless smog
Covering their bright eyes,
Long forgotten and misplaced.

Life from afar seemed exciting
But in their cold eyes, hatred and betrayal
Burned with the light of a thousand supernova.

One by one they blink
And their light is lost,
Forever and all eternity black.

Replaced by the young
Who are cloaked in light,
Dancing with new ideas and inspirations,
Never a thought for those they replaced.

Time waits for none
And these stars are gone,
Forgotten and dark,
No longer shining.

Ichabod Mills (16)
Ormiston Rivers Academy, Burnham-On-Crouch

WHAT SWANS ARE

Swans are proud, majestic creatures
They are a bright light on a dark night
They are loving birds
They float gracefully on a grey lake.

Swans are bright white snowflakes
They are clouds in a grey sky
They are the final blossom on an old tree
They are the sun on a cloudy day.

Swans are doves among ravens
They are horses running on a sandy beach
They are the moon on a starless night
Finally, they are caring and powerful.

That's what swans are.

Megan Robinson (13)
Ormiston Rivers Academy, Burnham-On-Crouch

LIFE AT SCHOOL

School is like a big dream,
School is like a football team,
School is as fun as a clown,
School is like a pronoun.

School is like a jail,
School is like blackmail,
School is as hard as a rock,
School is like a stopped clock.

School is as crowded as a stadium,
School is like an ice cream.

Hannah Shelley (12)
Ormiston Rivers Academy, Burnham-On-Crouch

GROWING UP

A mother's touch,
A book of pictures,
Piecing together my first puzzle,
The innocence of childhood, untainted by the world,
Reaching out to touch a bubble at my first 3D movie,
Scribbling on a page,
And being praised for my art,
The limitless love of a parent.

Shirt, skirt, shoes, tie,
Suddenly Mum's not there anymore,
Scribbling on a page,
No, that's not allowed,
The teacher cares, right?

Join your handwriting,
Your grades are too low!
She's perfect,
Be more like her,
Revise, revise!
Your results are your future!
But all I see are numbers.

Red pen is sandpaper,
Smoothing the edges of who you are
Flat, static, mature,
The colours of childhood

Washed away by a monotone world,
Turning creativity into ones and zeros.

Congratulations, you have a degree!
You are now the perfect shape
To fit into a world
Of nouns and full stops.
Your exclamation marks wasted away.

Skye Salek-Haddadi (12)
Roding Valley High School, Alderton Hill

THE STAGE OF LIFE

On the stage of life, we take a bow,
We tell ourselves we are ready now,
We're not really ready to face our fears,
All we're ready for are tears,
I know deep down I'm sick of this race,
Of exploring this universe at snail's pace,
Or do you want to wait for the storm,
After the controversy's formed?
Because I'm sick of judging people on their looks,
Reading their covers and not their books,
Screaming at them if their grades are too low,
It's about the test and not what we know,
Let's watch our world go into oblivion,
The rise and fall of the world we're living in,
Because people want money, cars and toys,
I just want to be paid in joy,
I want things to change but I don't want fame,
Somehow things still stay the same,
But whatever, friend, I'll see you around,
In a different city, a different town.

Poppy Tribe (11)
Roding Valley High School, Alderton Hill

WAKE UP WORLD

Why can't we have a world that is clean and green?
It's obscene!
We have ruthlessly polluted
When we have commuted
To work and to school and anywhere
We could have easily walked to.
Why do we have to be so stupid?
We've created too much rubbish
And been so sluggish in cleaning it all up.
I've had enough.
The air is smoky,
Our voices are croaky,
It's making us less healthy
But we have yet to notice.
Still, we say we are devoted and have promoted
Keeping the Earth clean...
When will the ignorance end?

Carys Gooding (12)
Roding Valley High School, Alderton Hill

UNDER MY FLOORBOARDS

I loved someone who didn't belong to me,
He's got me locked up and has the key.
I guess this love was never really true,
Before too long he said we were through.

It didn't last long,
Now it feels like my heart's being stomped on.
I've been shaken inside,
Been wiped out with the tide.

Now I wonder if what I've done
Was terribly wrong,
Under my floorboards.
He really is gone...?

Amber Elizabeth Compton (12)
Roding Valley High School, Alderton Hill

EVACUEE

Sadly I walk along the bustling station platform,
Through weeping mothers
And shouting teachers, to my class.
My younger sisters bounce along beside me.
I feel empty inside.

Before I turn the corner
I take one last look at my mother.
"Stay together!" she shouts.
The teacher bundles us onto the train.
I take a seat next to a sniffling child.
I let my sisters sit next to me,
They are all I have left.

It is raining
Raindrops as big as the lump in my throat.
As the train pulls away from the station,
I am broken-hearted.

Anna Broadbent (12)
Saffron Walden County High School, Saffron Walden

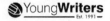

A SCHOOL DAY

The day starts with the same old boring lesson,
The day starts with the starter task
which sometimes causes depression,
With people screaming and with people shouting
it always hurts your head,
When they keep talking and you want silence
you kinda wish you were dead,
Finally some peace and quiet, everyone has calmed down
And whenever they start chatting again,
it makes the teacher frown.

Next is the second lesson, almost halfway through the day,
Oh wait, it's still the boring part,
come on, where's the holiday?
Well, since science is quite boring
I'm better off doing some work,
Now I need to answer tonnes of questions
using this old textbook,
I started the work and I didn't think it would be so hard,
OMG, I can't believe it, it's lunchtime at last!

Finally the last lesson, the last one of the day,
All the hard work presented in our books in many different
ways,
There's maths to do, one of my favourite lessons,
Please don't tell me this is gonna cause more depression,

Now it's the end of the day, no more mind games,
Oh no, kill me now, I just remembered tomorrow is another
day!

Keira Star (12)
The Harris Academy, Rainham

EXPECTATIONS

Expectations are huge,
your identity is hidden in a cape of fear,
not knowing what people will say or do
or their reactions to you.

Will they laugh? Make you feel small?
Judge you with every word
or whisper quickly to their group of popularity?

Your fear of imperfection rises,
you start to sweat off your make-up,
revealing the other layer.

As you finish speaking, you freeze,
no noise, no movement,
you already know the rumours, the *lies*.
People saying you want attention
but realising that they don't care,
you walk from the stage,
full of confidence and pride.

Caitlin Turner (13)
The Harris Academy, Rainham

GRANDAD - MISSING YOU

I know we are all feeling really sad,
That we lost our grandad, a friend and a dad.
Together we have cried an ocean of tears,
As we feel so empty and hold many fears.
But Grandad would want us to know he is in a good place,
And that he is watching us all with a smile upon his face.
As we made him so proud, as proud as can be,
That he has raised such a beautiful and special family.
Thinking back now, I must really say,
I feel lucky and privileged to have known Grandad to this day.
For in life he played a special part,
The memories I will treasure and keep close to my heart.
Grandad, although you have gone, we'll always be together,
And your spirit will live on in each one of us, forever.
If you are still here listening, please say a prayer for us every day,
Be sure to protect us and guide us on our way.
We know when God called you, you had to go,
But we want you to know, Gramps, we love you and miss you so.
Dear God, if it isn't too much fuss,
Take extra special care of our pops, for he is very dear to us.
A man of honour, dignity and pride.

Melina Tiwari (14)
The Harris Academy, Rainham

PERFECT

You look past me,
You push me aside,
It hurts...

You can say I'm crazy,
You can say I have lost my mind,
Yes, I may be ugly,
As ugly as a toad,
But I am still a person,
One that shouldn't be disguised,
I may not be what you call perfection,
But I am me,
The me that I love to be.

You look past me,
You push me aside,
It hurts...

I try to fit in,
I try to stay strong,
But I never succeed,
I don't know where I belong.
An emotional roller coaster twists in my head,
Bringing tears to my eyes,
I will never be what you call perfection,
But I shall always be me,
And there will be no changing me.

You look past me,
You push me aside,
It hurts...

But then I realise,
No one is better than me
At the challenge of which is hardest.
Being me is an everyday struggle that I face,
But I count on myself as I would my family.
I get myself through tough times.

I am perfect, no matter what you say.

Mia Brown (12)
The Harris Academy, Rainham

WHEN A LITTLE ONE COMES INTO YOUR LIFE...

As the contractions started everyone was so excited
for this new baby to arrive in the world.
The new mother was rushed into hospital,
waiting for the pain to end.

The new mother pushed and pushed
Whilst squeezing her husband's hand
The baby was finally born
The midwife tied a band around the baby girl's hand.

After an hour had passed
The mother and baby had bonded really fast
Everyone had a hold of the little baby
But she started to cry as she wanted her daddy.

As she got home and settled in
She got more visitors coming in
Each one of them said
She was a sweet as a button.

But when she cried
The tears escaped her eyes

Everyone said, "Ahhh,"
After seeing her.

She makes everyone so happy
Even when some are in a bad mood
Because she loves meeting new people
And she loves making them happy as she does with her
family.

Alice Hope (12)
The Harris Academy, Rainham

LIFE

First, it grows from a baby
A baby that needs to be made stable with two sticks and
tape
Then a young grown-up
Almost fifteen times bigger than a McDonald's cup.

Growing and growing, faster than The Flash
Growing and growing, until it crashed

Every winter is a struggle
Especially for the tall and strong old oak tree
It swishes and sways left to right, almost like a kite
It shrinks every single night.

It's far apart from its friends
It is getting old and losing strength
It will fight and fight until the very end.

Twigs and sticks all fall off onto the floor
It's lived too long, it is too tough to stay strong
It's weak and it's breaking, it can't go on anymore.

The birds sing, the tree cries
Just beginning to realise
His body is broken
He is no more
He is dead from the bottom of his core.

Immanuel Kotey (13)
The Harris Academy, Rainham

OUR GENERATION

This is your world, my world, our world,
if we don't change it, it's going to destroy your dreams
and destroy our world.

"This week, about 57 people between ages 12 and 20
were stabbed to death all around the United Kingdom."

The word 'united' should mean being together,
helping each other and motivating each other.

'Kingdom' is another word for community,
a word we should all come together for,
as family, brothers and sisters.

A knife should not be used for protection,
our words should, by saying "Stop," "Shake hands," or
"We can solve this by having a conversation."

Victoria-Enemwingue Idahosa-Obazee (13)
The Harris Academy, Rainham

SUCCEEDING IN LIFE

Life is not a thing to be wasted, life is precious.
One thing my dad always said to me was,
"To have a good life, you must excel.
If you want money, you need to work for it."
One thing I hated the most was reading.
One day my aunt said,
"If you want to excel, you have to study and read.
Readers are leaders."
My ambition is to be an aerospace engineer
But this will not happen if I choose the wrong path.
Life is full of obstacles
Obstacles that you must overcome
to open the gate to opportunities.
However, it is your choice.
Choose wisely and you will
definitely overcome these obstacles.

Victor Adablah (13)
The Harris Academy, Rainham

I'M NOT DIFFERENT

I'm gay, but this doesn't mean
I am different, I am still human.
Being gay doesn't mean
you can harass me
or kick me until I'm down.
I believe that anyone can be
who they want to be and
if that means them being
attracted to the same gender
then fine.

Life can get tough
but just remember that
life is like a piece of string,
there are many possibilities,
all good in their own ways.

It is normal, not disgusting.
As the people of the world
we should be more accepting
of anyone, no matter what
race, skin, religion or gender.

Alex Avery (13)
The Harris Academy, Rainham

THE BAD BOY

"Stop it!" they shout.
"Stop it you fool!"
If they just showed an interest in me
I could be the person they want me to be.

"Get outside!" I hear,
"You're just being lazy!"
They don't understand, I need help,
I am just a puppy that wants to yelp.

"I didn't do it."
"It wasn't me."
I just want to succeed and achieve
And I want my teachers to believe.

"I can do it!" I scream.
"I'm not bad!"
I just want to get the work done.

Kajus Proskinas (13)
The Harris Academy, Rainham

EVOLUTION OF LIFE

Life is a concept full of different obstacles
Hurdles we try to beat
It might be hard but we don't give up
We try and strive for an easy life but is that the answer?
We question life to ask why it punishes us for things we
can't do
By putting more hurdles in our way.

We start off as little babies
With no dreams or desires
But as we grow and develop
We start to work and have a belief
That we can become what we want to be.
That's the evolution of life.

Adrian Davidson (12)
The Harris Academy, Rainham

MY IMPERFECT ROLE MODEL

She isn't famous
She isn't poor
She has opportunities knocking at her door.

She isn't lost
She isn't found
You never know when she's coming round.

She isn't good
She isn't bad
But you will definitely know when she's going mad.

She is strong
She is pretty
She is amazing
She is my nan.

She is thunder
I am lightning.

She is the Batman
I am Robin.

She is the spider
I am the web.

And even though she is my nan
She is still my best friend.

Charlotte Luggar (11)
The Harris Academy, Rainham

I WATCH... I WAIT...

I watch, I wait,
Every day,
For my father to return.
I work every day
To return his pay.
Will he ever
Return from those trenches?
Will he return to me?
I miss him.
Deep, dark war.
War is harsh,
Lots of death, I hate it.
I want my father,
They stole him.
I sent to him.
No reply.
Is he alive?
I wonder.
I love him,
And want him home
In my arms.
I watch, I wait,
Every day,
For my father to return.

Jack Moorey (12)
The Harris Academy, Rainham

CATS

Cats are mysterious
Cats are fun
Cats sleep anywhere
Especially in the sun.

Their food is kinda smelly
But it fills their bellies
And after a long wander
You find them over yonder.

Water is their fear
And brings them to a tear
What makes them feel better
Is when they're away from the weather.

Something smells fishy
So you know to look for kitty
But look at the pretty little kitty
Because I love her so.

Bethany Debono (13)
The Harris Academy, Rainham

ANTISOCIAL

"Why are you awkward?
You seem physically well."
Today I have the answer:
I'm coming out of my shell.

For years I've felt dreadful
From socialisation, I hide.
I lost all my charisma,
Rage built up inside.

I thought I was simply shy,
I asked myself to hide me.
How was I suppose to know,
I had social anxiety?

I cut off my friends,
Which made my mind further decay.
"You seem so down," they stated,
"I'm fine," I'd say.

Adults didn't help me,
They made me feel stupid.
"You can't be this ill.
You're just a kid."

I'm trying my hardest to improve,
But I'm still going downhill.
How was I supposed to know,
I was mentally ill?

Elliot Crimes (13)
Thomas Lord Audley School, Monkwick

BULLIES

I hate when you take the mick,
And when you do, it makes me sick.
You steal my heart, which makes you a thief,
And I don't understand why you give so much grief.
All I do is sit in silence,
In return, I get verbal violence!
What I do, what I play,
What I like and what I say... they don't matter.
You're always horrible and ever so mean,
It seems like, to bully, you are keen.
However, my opinion doesn't matter,
I get told to ignore you,
But how? I don't have a clue.
You think you're better and bigger,
And every insult is as if you've pulled the trigger.
Like I say, this is me,
I like what I see.
My life is up to me, not you,
From now on, you don't tell me what to do!

Ashleigh Oldfield (12)

Thomas Lord Audley School, Monkwick

WHO CARES ABOUT SOCIAL MEDIA?

Why does everyone care about
how they appear on social media?
Instagram, Snapchat,
I'm personally done with all that.

Everyone is so much more mean,
especially when they're blinded by a computer screen.

Let's get on to racism.
Some people think that because you're from
a different country, you think about terrorism.

Forget about that,
because we know you are better than all of them!

If you have resilience
and also show perseverance,
you can be the best,
so much better than the rest.

Do you care how you appear
on social media and everywhere?

Tyler Riley (13)
Thomas Lord Audley School, Monkwick

I AM A WOMAN...

Why do you treat us differently?
Just like you, we aspire to be
strong, brave, proud and loved.
Proud of the women who look down from above
"You can't do it because you're a girl."
"Don't even try, you will just fail and cry."
Why?
We will fight just as hard
We will sing just as loud
Because women are strong, powerful and proud
Together we stand
hand in hand
Don't let people tell you that you can't
Tell them you can!
Shout it loud
Scream it out
Because you are a woman
Say it proud...
"I am a woman!
"I am glad!"

Megan Curtis (13)
Thomas Lord Audley School, Monkwick

DON'T BE AFRAID

You and I are the same is what you think,
But do you really know who I am?
You may think I'm perfect but actually, I'm hiding,
In the shadows, I hide away,
I explore the darkness all around us,
I wear black and cover my face with my hair,
You don't know this because I hide myself,
I hide myself so I'm not afraid,
I hide myself so people like you don't comment or laugh,
But now I know to not care,
To show people who I really am,
To express what I believe and what I don't,
To know I'm unique and to love myself,
For I know who I am and who I want to be.

Lana Hay (13)
Thomas Lord Audley School, Monkwick

AFTER SCHOOL

My PlayStation,
Usually turns on after school, I grab my controller,
And pick my character that looks the best,
Then I get into the lobby with 100 people,
That I'm about to kill,
I get a victory royale,
And get into another game,
Get another name,
But it's a shame,
I have to kill everyone,
Which makes me the best,
When I'm hiding in a bush,
My team tells me to shush,
Or I'll give my spot away,
Might undo the play,
I would like to be the best,
That would be my dream,
Do you understand what I mean?

Lewis Robert Bowyer (13)
Thomas Lord Audley School, Monkwick

MOTHER EARTH

We have started to hurt her,
When we should help her nurture,
We destroy the atmosphere,
When we should keep it clear,
Because if we end up losing her,
We can't get a new one of her,
She is the only one we've got,
Even though she isn't a lot,
We pollute her and we dilute her,
I just wonder why we loot her,
And why we rid her of her possessions,
As if we are starting to hurt her,
When we should help her nurture.

Freddie Baker (13)
Thomas Lord Audley School, Monkwick

WOMEN HAVE RIGHTS

Women have rights,
Just like men.
We are strong,
We are proud,
We have the power to rule the world.

Women have rights,
Just like men.
We are beautiful,
We are brave,
We shouldn't have any need to be afraid.

Women have rights,
Just like men.
We are great,
We are loved,
We are the people from above.

Women have rights,
Just like men.
There's no need for the hate
That there has been.

Aimee Georgina Wood (13)
Thomas Lord Audley School, Monkwick

CONCRETE JUNGLE

Trees and plants everywhere,
Growing tall and breathing air,
Then comes man to chop them down,
To make way for urban towns,
Not giving thought to Mother Nature,
Or what was given by our creator,
It's now that we need to change,
Give back what we take,
It is up to us to change our ways,
For our planet to see brighter days.

Napat Menic Tawanyarat (13)
Thomas Lord Audley School, Monkwick

IT'S ONLY A MATTER OF TIME

You have to be perfect! He wants you to.
Put up with it a little longer. It's only a matter of time.
Fake a smile, maybe, even a laugh.
Look believable. Make it real.
But remember, it's only a matter of time.

Oh! Don't forget about school, it's no different.
Shut them out, it's only a matter of time.
Try to make friends and try to fit in. Just try. Try harder.
At least try to look believable.
Just remember, it's only a matter of time

When you get home, try to look normal.
Whatever normal is, it's only a matter of time.
Do what he tells you to do. No is not an option.
At least try to look believable. Try. Try harder.
Just remember, it's only a matter of time

Cover up. Don't let anyone see the marks.
He told you what could happen if they do. It's only a matter of time.
For how long? Forever? The truth will come out. It always does!
It's only a matter of time.

Oreoluwa Akinwunmi (13)
Westcliff High School For Girls, Westcliff-On-Sea

WE REFUGEES

We refugees we aren't safe,
We don't know where we came from,
We don't know where we are going,
But we've got to push.

Home is supposed to be the place you feel safe,
Well we didn't,
That's why we are here,
But where is that?

Each day we don't know what challenges are ahead,
Hiding from those who feel we are outsiders,
We are, aren't we?

Immigrants, that's what they call us,
We don't cause harm,
But we are still hiding from it.

We refugees we aren't safe,
We don't know where we came from,
We don't know where we are going,
But we are still one of you.

Ade Hikmat Kosoko (12)
Westcliff High School For Girls, Westcliff-On-Sea

SHE STOOD THERE ALONE

She stood there alone
Whilst the rest of the world
Sat with their friends,
Played games with no end,
Laughed at funny jokes,
Drank cans of diet Coke,
She stood there alone.

Whilst the rest of the world
Giggled on their phones,
Trudged to school with a moan,
Played a game of ball,
Tried to look cool,
She stood there alone.

Whilst the rest of the world
Celebrated birthdays,
Travelled on holidays,
Spent all their money,
Went to a new country,
She stood there alone.

Though she had once had fame
Had lived a life with no pain

But she had thrown it away,
With endless greed,
And terribly bad deeds,
Which meant she stood there alone.

Isabelle O'Dell (12)
Westcliff High School For Girls, Westcliff-On-Sea

DEPTH OF PERCEPTION OF YOU AND ME

Culture be damned
On the path I walk.
Religion is but another land
From the one where I was taught.
Nationality is just equal
My own ideas fought
Gender devolving
Acceptance wasn't sought.

Because my mind is absolute
In the memories forged.
My heart is resolute
From the trials, I launched.

Years of torture and torment,
Of heartfelt heartbreak
And darkness and mistake.

And although I know no one is truly free,
I, in the traditional sense, am still me.
These masks that chafe,
No one can see.

So throw it away; be true to yourself.
Or instead, follow your hollow path.

Edward Maclannan-Brown (17)
Westcliff High School For Girls, Westcliff-On-Sea

 YoungWriters
— Est. 1991 —

YOUNG WRITERS
INFORMATION

We hope you have enjoyed reading this book – and
that you will continue to in the coming years.

If you're a young writer who enjoys reading and creative
writing, or the parent of an enthusiastic poet or story writer,
do visit our website **www.youngwriters.co.uk**. Here you will
find free competitions, workshops and games, as well as
recommended reads, a poetry glossary and our blog.

If you would like to order further copies of this book,
or any of our other titles, then please give us
a call or visit **www.youngwriters.co.uk**.

Young Writers
Remus House
Coltsfoot Drive
Peterborough
PE2 9BF
(01733) 890066
info@youngwriters.co.uk

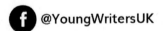 @YoungWritersUK    @YoungWritersCW